You Are Royal

Written By: Katelyn Artman

Illustrated By: Amber Lewis

You Are Royal

Scripture quotations are taken from the Holy Bible.
New International Version, NIV.

Edited by Lynda Dietz

To my beautiful children, Arco, Emmeline, and Eli. I pray that you will always know you are children of the One True King.

You are wanted. You are loved. Your are His.
You are Royal.

I love you to pieces,
Mom

Did you know that you're a
prince or princess, little one?
You will see why I say this
before this book's done.

1

We all have heard stories of big stone castles,

and long flowy dresses and robes with tassels.

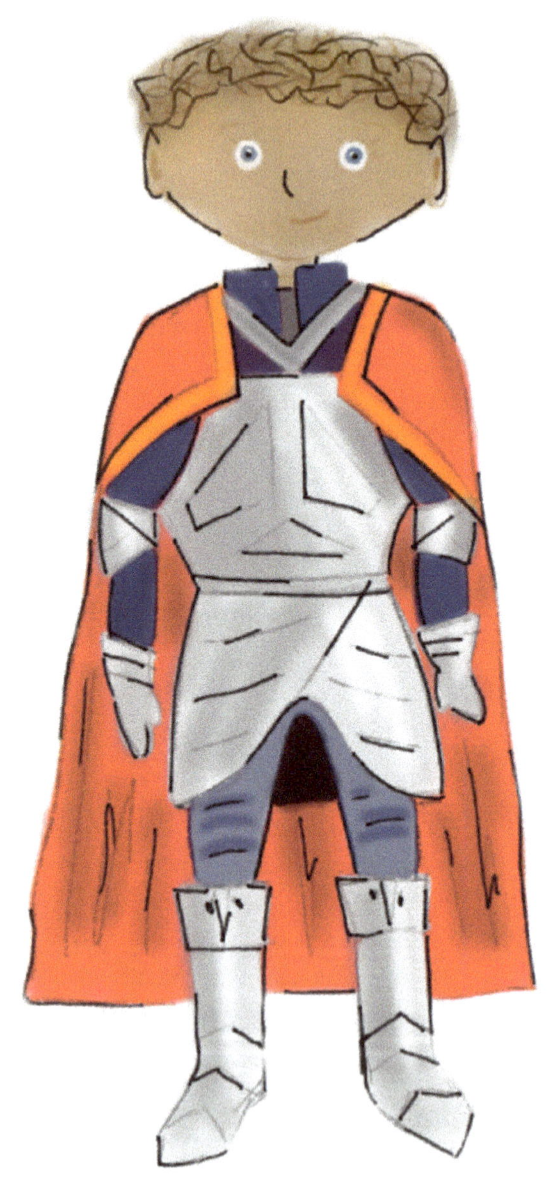

Movies are made with strong princes and knights,

and beautiful princesses who shimmer in lights.

I bet you thought nobles were only in books, but the truth's in the Bible, so let's take a good look.

2 Timothy 3:16-17

God has many names in His Word, you see.
He's the Heavenly Father to you and to me.

God is our Father,
but He's also a King!

So that makes us royal,
and that makes us sing:

Psalm 9:2

I am a prince. He makes me strong and brave.
I will tell everyone He has beaten the grave!

I am a princess. I'm wonderfully made.
God is my Father so I'm not afraid.

If you ever have doubts about
who you are, remember,
you're God's child wherever
you are.

He knit you together and calls you by name. He loves you, so He left His throne and came.

He came down to this earth
to bring light into darkness.
To save us from our yucky
sin and our mess.

John 8:12
John 3:17

If we say He is Lord and in our hearts we believe,
then He will freely forgive us and His gifts we'll receive.

We'll live in His Castle with Him someday,
wearing crowns on our heads, singing praise every day.

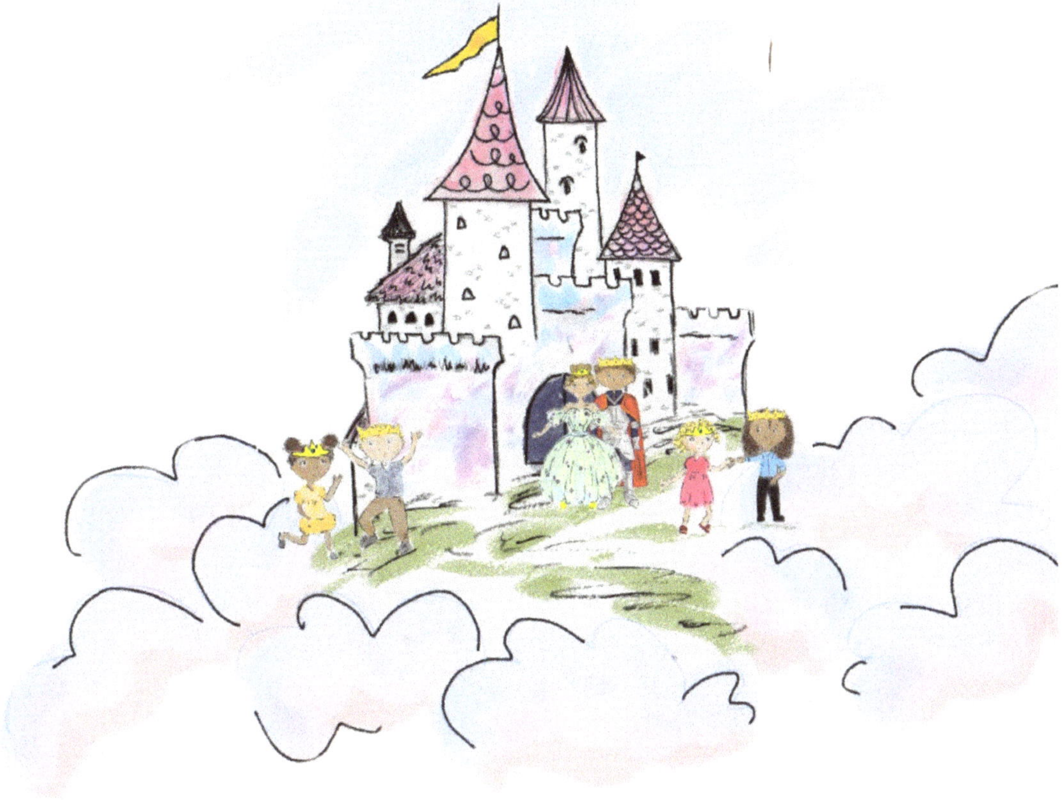

Psalm 9:2

So there is a song that we can now sing,
because God is our Father and He is our King:

I am a prince. He makes me strong and brave.
I will tell everyone He has beaten the grave!

I am a princess. I'm wonderfully made.
God is my Father so I'm not afraid.

You see, you're so much more
than just one in the crowd.
You're Royal, my dear,
so shout it out loud!

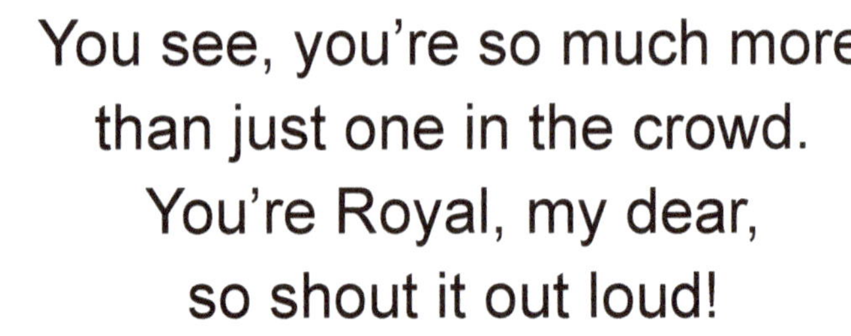

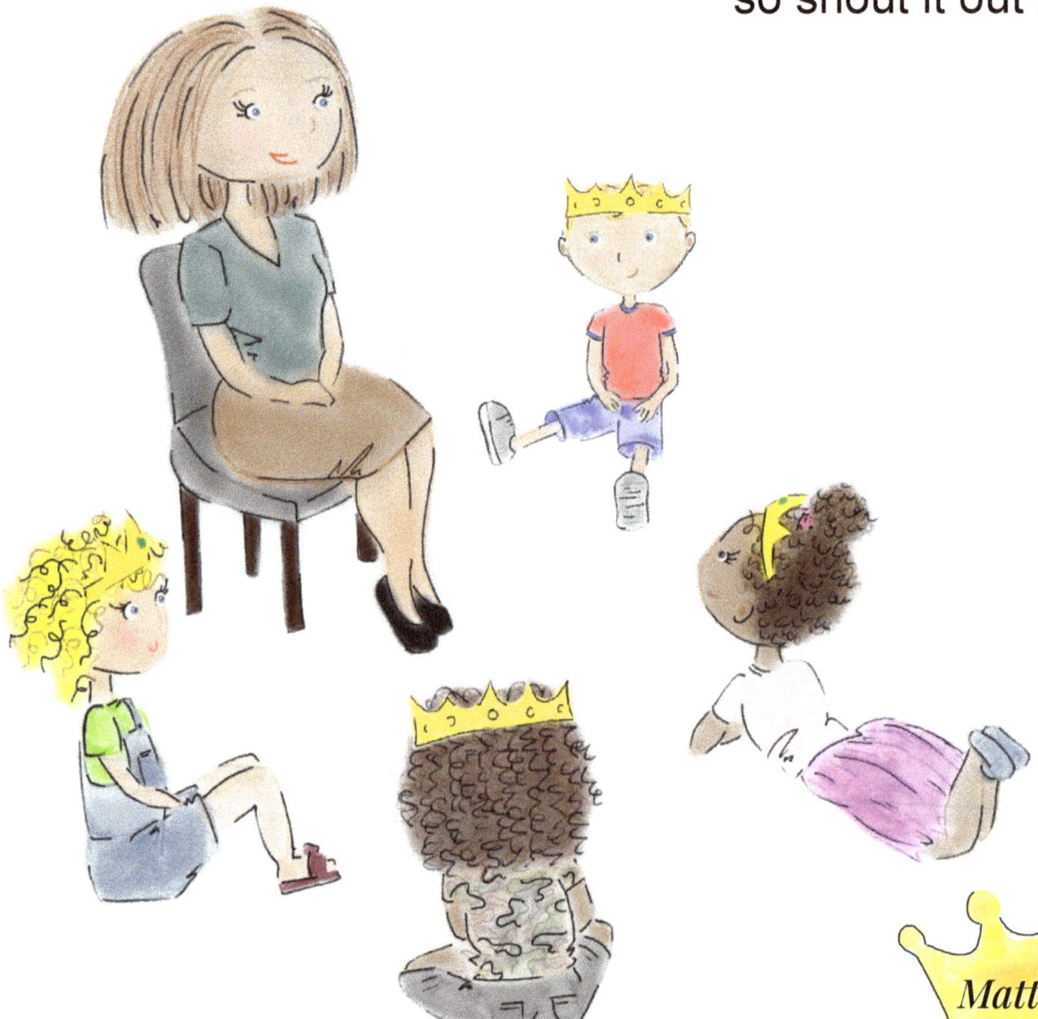

I Am Royal!

Scripture References Throughout the Book

Galatians 3:29

"If you are Christs', then you are Abraham's offspring, heirs according to promise."

2 Timothy 3:16-17

"All scripture is Breathed out by God and profitable for training in righteousness."

Psalm 24:10

"Who is this King of Glory, the Lord of Hosts, He is the King of Glory."

Mark 14:36

"And he said, "Abba,Father, All things are possible for You."

Psalm 9:2

"I will be glad and exalt in you. I will sing praise to your name, O Most High."

Isaiah 40:29

"He gives strength to the weary and increases the power of the weak."

Matthew 28:6

"He is not here, for he has risen.

Psalm 139:14

"I praise you- for I am fearfully and wonderfully made."

Isaiah 41:10

"Fear not, for I am with you. I will strengthen you, I will help you."

**Here are some ways
you can praise God:**

Singing

Drawing

Schoolwork

Playing

Sports

Chores

MATH

The Road to Becoming Royal

All people have sinned. Sin's Penalty is Death. Christ paid the penalty and created a bridge for us by dying on the cross. Salvation is the only way to become Royal—it's not by works. If you believe in Christ and confess it with your mouth that Jesus is Lord, then you will become Royal forever.

www.ingramcontent.com/pod-product-compliance
Lightning Source LLC
Chambersburg PA
CBHW042047140726
48006CB00020BA/2666